Time Gentlemen please . . .

The demise of the Sheffield Public House

The derelict Bell Hagg , Manchester Road

ISBN 781905278206
Printed in 2008 by Pickard Communication

Published by youbooks.com
11 Riverside Park, Sheaf Gardens, Sheffield S2 4BB
Telephone 0114 275 7222
www.youbooks.com

*Whilst every effort has been made to check the information on closures given in this book,
it may well be that some of the hostels mentioned (those still standing) will re-open.
Breweries, and individual buyers regularly decide to redevelop
a public house in areas that are being regenerated.*

Bull and Oak and the Brown Cow public houses in the Wicker - both now demolished to make way for Parkway to Shalesmoor relief road

Bridge Inn was sited near the junction of Weedon Street and Meadowhall Road - now demolished

Cannon Hall Hotel was situated in Fir Vale - now demolished

The Catherine Arms 29-31 Catherine Street, Burngreave - still standing but looking rather worse for wear

A good example of a Garrison Public house, the Rose Inn at 627 Penistone Road, Hillsborough was demolished to make way for the McDonalds fast food outlet. The building was used as a makeshift mortuary during the Great Sheffield Flood in the 1860s

The Alexandra Hotel, 549 Carlisle Street East, Sheffield. This public house closed in the mid 1970s

Now demolished the Cambridge Hotel stood at 452 Penistone Road, Hillsborough

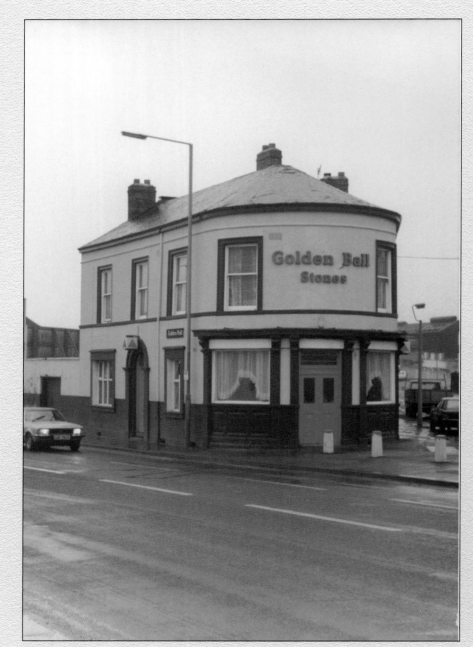 

The Golden Ball, 838 Attercliffe Road, Sheffield (aka Turnpike) was demolished in the early 1990s to make way for the Don Valley Stadium

The Crown Inn, 21 Meadowhall Road, Sheffield S9. Closed in 2008 when David Layne ex Sheffield Wednesday player decided to call a halt to his days as landord. The public house is still standing and hopefully may be re-opened

The Crow's Nest Hotel was on High Pavement, St John's Road, Hyde Park, Sheffield

Denison Arms, 33 Watery Street, 64 Malinda Street, Sheffield

Dog and Partridge, 575 Attercliffe Road, Sheffield 9

Domino, Egerton Stree, Sheffield - a short lived public house opened in the late 1960s or early 1970's and demolished less than 40 years later

Earl Francis Hotel, 64 Manor Oaks Road, Sheffield

The Earl George, 61 The Pavement, Sheffield

Enfield Arms, 95 Broughton Lane, Attercliffe, Sheffield demolished in early 2008. The pub was at one time owned by the Sheffield Steelers Hockey team

The Yorkshire Grey or Minerva Tavern or Bar Rio was demolished to make way for a hotel. Situated at 69 Charles Street, Sheffield

Woodthorpe Arms, 102 Mansfield Road, Intake, Sheffield - now demolished

The Engineers or Dallas Bar or Barrow House was ravaged by fire and demolished around 2007. Used to sell Berry's Lion Ale.

Excelsior, 1 Carbrook Street, Attercliffe Common, Sheffield was demolished in June 1993.

The Cricket Inn at 317 Cricket Inn Road was built in 1936. Demolished about 60 years later.

The Lambpool, 291 Attercliffe Common was built in 1870 and demolished in the mid 1990s

The Fox and Duck, 174 Pye Bank Road, or possibly 174 Pitsmoor Road, Sheffield

Royal Hotel stood on the corner of Bradfield Road and Penistone Road, Sheffield, facing the Owlerton Greyhound stadium - now demolished

The Magnet Hotel, Southey Green, Sheffield 5. Ted Catlin a Cup winner with Sheffield Wednesday was licensee at this pub in the 1940s. - now demolished

Crown Inn, 116 Neepsend Lane, Sheffield 3 - This pub was the tap for the Stones Brewery which stood just behind.

Halfway House, 80 Britannia Road, Darnall, Sheffield S9

Hare and Hounds, Church Street, Stanningon Village, Sheffield - the building is still standing awaiting property development

Hare and Hounds, Uppergate Road, Stanningon Village, Sheffield - the pub was the predecessor to the pub on page 30. Built in 1837 and demolished in 1960s

Haychatter was previously known as the Reservoir Inn. Situated in Bradfield Dale, Bradfield.

Highway, Fox Street, Pitsmoor, Sheffield built in the 1960s

The Norfolk Arm, 160 Attercliffe Road, Sheffield S4, opened in 1840 - has now been closed as a pub for about 25 years

Horseshoe Inn 279 Bellhouse Road, Shiregreen, Sheffield - now demolished

Huntsman, 975 Barnsley Road, Sheffield, demolished in 2008 to make way for apartments

The Jervis Lum, Park Grange Drive, Sheffield S2

Jolly Buffer, 144 Ecclesall Road, Sheffield 11

The King's Head, Manchester Road, Sheffield 10, demolished to make way for more apartments

Lansdowne Hotel, 2 Lansdowne Road, London Road, Sheffield 11. The pub closed in early 1990s - now demolished

Link Hotel, 338 Hague Row, Sheffield

The Industry Inn, 89 Main Road and the Meadow Inn at 81 Main Road, Darnall. Both buildings are still standing but no longer selling beer

Meadow Street Hotel, 110 Meadow Street, Sheffield. This pub was built in the first half of the 19th century.

Midland Hotel 2 Alfred Road, Sheffield - situated near the junction of Newhall Road and Brightside Lane

Albion Hotel, Mill Tavern, Old Mill Tavern at 2-4 Earsham Street, Pitsmoor, Sheffield 4. Now part of the John Heath Funeral Directors

Moseley's Arms, 81-83 West Bar, Sheffield 3, This public house was originally named the Rose until in 1829 Thomas Moseley took over, hence the name change.

Nags Head, 325 Shalesmoor, Sheffield. Demolished for road widening purposes in 2006

The New White Lion 23 The Wicker, Sheffield is now used as a fishing tackle shop

The Ball Inn 287 Darnall Road, Sheffield 9 built around 1910

Newfield Inn, 141 Denmark Road, Sheffield S2

Hole in Wall, aka Wicker Brewery tap, 70 Savile Street, Sheffield S3 - now demolished

The Durham Ox, 15 Cricket Inn Road, Sheffield 2

Normanton Springs Hotel, 65 Normanton Springs Road, Sheffield - now demolished

Old Blue Ball, 67 Broad Street, Sheffield - now demolished

Old Bowling Green Hotel, 2 Upwell Lane, Grimesthorpe, Sheffield

Britannia Inn 24-26 Worksop Road, Attercliffe, Sheffield - may well open again?

Royal Oak , 11 Hollis Croft, West Bar, Sheffield - now demolished

Old Light Horseman, 155 Penistone Road, Sheffield - now demolished

Pike and Heron, Bawtry Road, Tinsley, Sheffield

Players Cafe, Attercliffe Common, Sheffield - Still standing but not longer licenced premises - use to be the old Carbrook Elementary School 5-11 year olds.

Plumpers, 42 Greystock Road, 36 Sutherland Road, Norfolk Bridge, Sheffield - now demolished

Plumpers Hotel, Sheffield Road, and 200 Bawtry Road, Sheffield - sited near to the Tinsley/Meadowhall Junction. Now being used as a golf equipment shop

Queens Head, 606 Attercliffe Road, Attercliffe, Sheffield. On the corner of Shirland Lane - still standing but only just!

Queens Hotel, 85 Scotland Street, Sheffield S3 - still standing but boarded up

Ratteners Rest, Globe Buildings, Penistone Road, Shalesmoor area of Sheffield

The Viaduct at 79 the Wicker and Station Hotel at 95 the Wicker are now closed - These two were amongst the ten public houses that used to adorn the Wicker area

Robin Hood, 46-48 Ellesmere Road, Sheffield

Roman Ridge, Roman Ridge Road, Sheffield - the name serves to remind us of earlier times when the Roman Empire ruled Britain for over 500 years.

Rose and Crown, 245 Main Street, Darnall, Sheffield 9

Royal Hotel, 1 Abbeydale Road, Sheffield 7 - now developed as the Royal apartments

The Royal Lancers, 66-68, Penistone Road, Sheffield 6

Old Blue Bell, 120 Worksop Road, Attercliffe, Sheffield S9 - this building is now used as a mosque

Adelphi Hotel, 13 Arundel Street, Sheffield - the Crucible Theatre now stands on this site. Both Sheffield football clubs originated from meetings at this establishment

Shiregreen Hotel, 416 Sicey Avenue, Sheffield - built in 1939 and now derelict.

Sicey Hotel, Sicey Avenue, Shiregreen, Sheffield - now demolished

Sign Post, 31 Andover Street, Pitsmoor, Sheffield

The Sportsmans Group, 851 Penistone Road, Sheffield 6 - now demolished

The Station Hotel, The Wicker, Sheffield

The Talbot, aka Ye Old Toad, Good Doctor, 40 Hoyle Street, Sheffield 3
now demolished

Bird in Hand, 49 Broughton Lane, Attercliffe, Sheffield 9 - this picture was taken just after closure when the premises was being used as a typesetting business, Forword Processing

Tea Gardens, aka Public Gardens, Saracens Head, Public Gardens, 88-90 Grimesthorpe Road, Sheffield 4

Staniforth Arms, 261 Staniforth Road, Sheffield 9 - now a restaurant

Three Tuns, 55 Leopold Street, Sheffield - now part of the Orchard Square complex

Travellers Rest 525 City Road, Sheffield

The Viaduct, 79 The Wicker, is now a business premises, which is a good thing as passing trade is now non-existent

The Albert, 31 Sutherland Street, Norfolk Bridge, Sheffield 4 - now demolished but at one time frequented by the Mooney and Garvin gangs of Sheffield

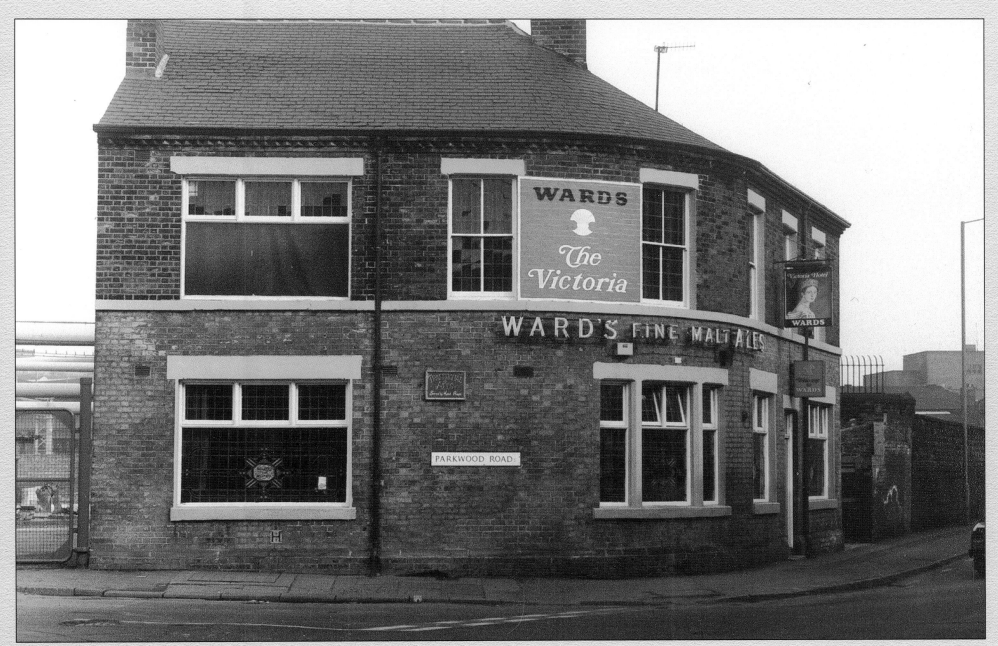

Victoria Hotel or Victoria Gardens, 248 Neepsend Lane, Sheffield - nicknamed the Monkey

Victoria Hotel, 923 Penistone Road, Hillsborough, Sheffield 6 - now demolished

Waggon and Horses, 2 Kent Road, 236 Gleadless Road, Sheffield - now derelict

Wellington Inn, 720 Brightside Lane, Sheffield 9 - now demolished

White Horse, 57 Malinda Street, Sheffield 3 - this pub is no longer standing but it was not demolished as such - it fell down whilst being renovated

White Swan, 105 Meadow Hall Road, Sheffield (aka Old White Swan) - now demolished

Tramcar 851 Attercliffe Road, Attercliffe, Sheffield - on the corner of Clay Street - now demolished. The gentleman on the photo is Ernest Wagstaff local shopkeeper

Broughton Inn, 1 Broughton Lane or 342 Attercliffe Common, Sheffield 9 - now demolished

Bulldog, aka Bridge, 387 Attercliffe Road, Washford Bridge, Sheffield 9 - Still standing hopefully to reopen but . . .

Furnival, Verdon Street, previously Verdun Street, Pitsmoor, Sheffield 3 - now used as a church meeting room

The Lion Hotel, aka Black Lion, 2 Nursery Street, Sheffield

New Inn, 108 Ecclesall Road, Sheffield - now demolished

Commercial, on the corner of Weedon Street and Sheffield Road, Carbrook, Sheffield 9. Now demolished.

Blake Hotel, aka Blake Street Hotel, 53 Blake Street, Sheffield 6

Bulls Head Hotel, 18 Dun Street, Shalesmoor, Sheffield 3 - This was one of three public houses on this small road. Queens, Gardners Rest being the other two

Harlequin, 26 Johnson Street, The Wicker, Sheffield 3

Bell Inn, Fitzalan Square, Sheffield

Bell Hagg Inn, Manchester Road, Sheffield 6

Pump Tavern, 79 South Street, 77 The Moor, Sheffield - now demolished

Junction, 354 Brightside Lane, Attercliffe, Sheffield 9. Situated on the corner with Newhall Road - now demolished

Photograph courtesy of Bernard Mettam

Tramway Hotel, 126 London Road, Sheffield 2

Tramway Hotel, 126 London Road, Sheffield 2

Photograph courtesy of Bernard Mettam

Twelve O Clock - 1 or 127 Attercliffe Road, Sheffield 9 - long since demolished used to stand facing the clock at Tommy Wards corner

Cross Daggers, 14 Market Place, Woodhouse, Sheffield

Lady's Bridge Hotel, on the corner of Bridge Street and Lady's Bridge, Sheffield

Photograph courtesy of Bernard Mettam

Gatefield Tavern built within the Kelvin Flats complex, 165 Infirmary Road, Sheffield 6 - now demolished along with the flats

Greyhound, 217 Gibraltar Street, Shalesmoor, Sheffield - now demolished

Old Library, aks Weetwood House, Ecclesall Road, Sheffield - a project that no one wanted - the conversion of an old library to a pub that no one visited - £2.3 millions spent in the process and it is now closed. All's well that ends well

The Hare and Hound, 27-29 Nursery Street, Sheffield 3 - now derelict

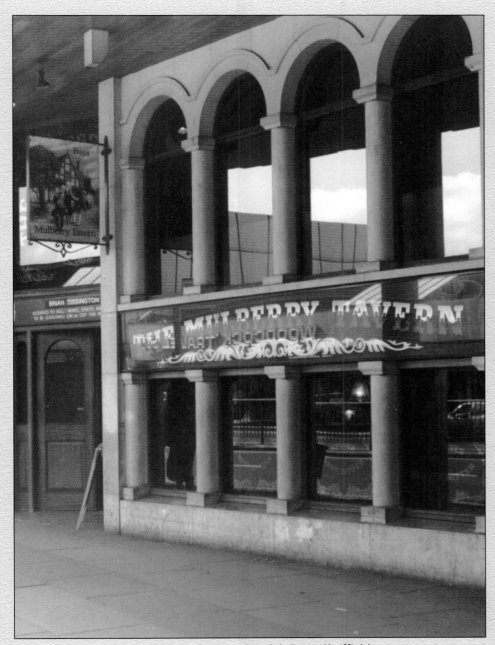

Mulberry Tavern, 2 Mulberry Street, or Arundel Gate, Sheffield

Saddle Inn, 94 West Street, closed early 1990s and moved 60 yards down West St.

Plough, 28 Broad Street, Sheffield - long since demolished

Pheasant 436 Attercliffe Common, Attercliffe, Sheffield 9 - the old building was demolished and the new Pheasant (now the Stumble Inn) built to replace it

Marples, aka London Mart, Commercial Hotel, 64 High Street, Sheffield. Many lives were lost on the night of 12th December 1940 during the Sheffield Blitz, over 75 people were killed when a German bomber scored a direct hit, flattening the pub.

Salutation Inn, 126 Attercliffe Common, on the corner of Coleridge Road, Sheffield - this cream tiled pub was long since demolished - The Pavilion cinema can be seen in the centre of the picture

Wharncliffe Arms, 42-44 West Street, Sheffield - William Abednego Thompson (The Great Bendigo) a prizefighter of note was once the landlord of this pub.

Whirlow Bridge Inn, Ecclesall, Bierlow, Sheffield

Golden Ball, Townhead Street, the original was built in 1825 - rebuilt on site pictured in 1900 and finally demolished and rebuilt on Campo Lane in the 1960s

Green Dragon, 469-471 Attercliffe Road, Sheffield 9 - sited near the junction of Attercliffe Road and Effingham Road - now demolished

The fire damages Norfolk Arms, Hollow Meadows